R. ALLEN BROWN

CASTLES

SHIRE ARCHAEOLOGY

Cover photograph
Raglan Castle, Gwent.
(Cadbury Lamb.)

British Library Cataloguing in Publication Data
Brown, R. Allen
Castles — (shire archaeology; 36)
1. Castles — England — History
I. Title
942 DA660
ISBN 0-85263-653-9

Published by
SHIRE PUBLICATIONS LTD
Cromwell House, Church Street, Princes Risborough,
Aylesbury, Bucks HP17 9AJ, UK

Series Editor: James Dyer

ISBN 0 85263 653 9

First published 1985

Set in 11 point Times and printed in Great Britain by
C. I. Thomas & Sons (Haverfordwest) Ltd,
Press Buildings, Merlins Bridge, Haverfordwest, Dyfed.

Contents

List of illustrations

1
Definition and function

Castles need to be defined before they can be understood. When all periods including the present produce fortification, what is it about the castle which makes it different from the rest and which confines it (as properly it should be confined) to the medieval period and (still more properly) to the feudal period? The answer is that the castle is a residential fortress, a seriously fortified residence. Further, it is the fortified residence of a lord, any lord, not necessarily the king or prince. It is this essential duality of residence and fortress which is evidently unique to the castle, and it is the private and seigneurial role that goes with it, as opposed to the communal one, that distinguishes the castle in the history of fortification. Thus in the West which is its context — and in England, let us say, from the coastal forts of Henry VIII onwards — all modern fortresses are exclusively military with no element of private residence. In earlier periods, on the other hand, all known types of fortification are communal, whether we think of iron age forts or Roman forts, Viking camps or Anglo-Saxon burghs. All these — and not least the Old English burghs of Alfred and his successors — may often develop into fortified communities, fortified towns and cities, and as such survive and flourish throughout the medieval period and beyond. But fortified towns and cities are clearly not castles, and the difference is made most obvious when in England, after 1066, the Normans planted their new and comparatively smaller castles in or beside the existing communal fortifications of London, York or Exeter, Pevensey, Hastings, Portchester or Old Sarum, and many other places.

The residential role of castles requires emphasis as no less fundamental than the military, though less well known. Even their siting was not determined exclusively by military considerations and most of those castles which survive in use, their military importance having withered away, do so as the stateliest of stately homes, as at Windsor and Arundel, Warwick and Alnwick. The fact that in France the word *château* is nowadays applied to any large house of pretension, though irritating to the traveller in search of castles, is of deep historical significance.

As for the military role of castles, it may be suggested that this is better known than understood. For it is not merely defensive. Certainly the defensive function largely controls the castle's form,

Fig. 1. Deal Castle, Kent, a Tudor coastal fort.

design and development; but in action, and in the warfare and thus the politics of the feudal period, its role and its military potential were at least as much offensive as defensive. The defensive spirit is not prominent in the ethos of the feudal warrior aristocracy, never so happy as when in the saddle, and the Normans did not fill Wales with castles because they were afraid of the Welsh. By means of the mounted men within it (who did not need their horses to defend the walls and towers) the castle could and did control the surrounding countryside. This was militarily what castles were for, and their range was the range of the horse. They were armed bases: they established, as we would say, a military presence; and he who would control the land (which is what medieval like other warfare is all about) must first control the castles. Hence all those sieges, and in them the castle's defensive strength was paramount. And because throughout the medieval period (gunpowder after about 1300 notwithstanding) defence in siegecraft was in the ascendant over attack, and because castle garrisons (an anachronistic word) were comparatively small yet immune from all save a full-scale and prolonged investment in an age when such operations were difficult to mount and sustain, we may begin to see the huge military importance of castles and why contemporaries gave them so much money and prestige.

The warfare of the feudal period was dominated by castles and by heavy cavalry, that is knights, and the two things went together, military-fashion, in that, while castles were the fortified bases especially of mounted men, a castle could not, on the other side, be taken by a cavalry charge.

These basic considerations bring us next to the essential feudality of castles. Feudalism was in origin all about knights, the provision, maintenance and training of this particularly expensive and therefore exclusive, type of warrior, with his costly warhorses and equipment, who required from early youth up a lifetime of dedication to horsemanship and the military arts and was as professional as the age could make him. Feudalism also was society organised for war — but warfare of a particular kind, namely mounted warfare. This does not mean that infantry was not used (there was more Norman infantry than cavalry at Hastings, for example) or was any more despised than it has been since by other arms, notably the cavalry; but it does mean that the

Fig. 2. Warwick Castle.

Fig. 3. Knights at Cressac (Charente, fresco). Based in castles, knights provided the offensive power by which a castle dominated the surrounding area.

knights were the *corps d'élite,* and the shock tactic of their charge with couched lance (held rigid under the arm, momentum of horse and rider thus concentrated at its point) was the ultimate weapon of feudal armies. This military élite inevitably became a social élite also, not least because of the horsemanship required ('You can make a horseman of a lad at puberty: later than that never,' according to a Carolingian proverb), and if not all knights were or could become great men, the association of knighthood and gentility started early, and all great men were knights.

By this route, then, we meet our feudal aristocracy. Feudal society was, whatever else, aristocratic, and dominated by a military and militant aristocracy. It is not unique in that respect; but its ruling class were not merely warriors but mounted warriors, and its ethos not merely military but equestrian to boot. The concepts of chivalry were born of the feudal period and, if words have any meaning, you cannot be chivalrous without a horse. Perhaps already, then, we may begin to see that the castle is essentially feudal. All architecture reflects both the needs and the aspirations of that society which produces it. Nothing could seem more appropriate than that the military and mounted aristocracy of, say, the tenth to the fifteenth centuries, should have found its preferred domestic setting in the fortified residence which was the castle, symbolically dominating the surrounding countryside, and doing so in practice by means of the knights who were the military contingent of the lord's household.

Fig. 4. The keep of Lavardin Castle, Loire-et-Cher, France.

To architectural symbolism we shall briefly return, but meanwhile the feudality of the castle can be amply demonstrated by date. For it evidently belongs exclusively to the feudal period as the characteristic architectural expression of that society in the West which we for other reasons dub 'feudal'. Though there can clearly be no divine law which prohibits anything so obvious as a defended residence from occurring in any other time or place (which may perhaps leave room for the odd Goltho, and even a *rath* or two), if we look for the origins of castles proper, that is of the seriously fortified residences of lords, we find them in the late ninth, and more clearly the tenth century, in the kingdom of the West Franks and in the break-up of Carolingian monarchy, which is precisely when and where we also find the origins of feudal society itself, based upon local lordship. At the other end of the castle's chronological span, we find its decline, the falling away of its military importance, which was half its *raison d'être* and what distinguished it from unfortified lordly residences, in the sixteenth and seventeenth centuries, as an integral part of the decline of feudalism as the state came increasingly to be organised by other means (more modern but also more ancient) than the feudal bond binding lord and vassal in a nexus of homage and fealty, tenure and service.

In between, closely controlled by the king or prince, whether directly his or held by his vassals, castles were the pillars of society and the focal points of medieval polity — 'the keys of the kingdom' as William of Newburgh wrote of the royal castles in the England of Henry II. As the residences of the great, the centres of military power, the centres also of local government, of rents and services, there is no doubt that castles stood for lordship in men's minds and were much of its substance also. 'You shall have the lordship' [of the northern counties], said the envoys of the Young King, seeking to win over the king of Scots to their enterprise against the same Henry II; 'you shall have the lordship in castle and in tower.' And the contemporary word applied to those great towers, which rise above so many castles as what the French would call the *pièce maitresse* of the whole building, was *donjon,* derived from the Latin *dominium* meaning lordship.

2
Origins

The earliest castles known to survive are those of Langeais, usually dated to about 994, and Doué-la-Fontaine, dated to about 950. The former is attributed to Fulk Nerra ('the Black'), count of Anjou, and the latter, probably, to Theobald, count of Blois. In the case of Doué-la-Fontaine the spectacular excavations of 1967-70 revealed the origin of the castle as a late Carolingian lordly residence; an unfortified, stone-built ground-floor hall of about 900 was converted fifty years later (having been burnt out in war) into a defensive but residential tower by the addition of an upper storey, its ground-floor entrances rigorously blocked. Langeais, too, has a masonry and residential tower as its principal building and strength. Both are in northern France and the area of the Loire valley, and both pertain precisely to the period of the establishment of feudal society and of the great comital families with their feudal principalities into which France was to be divided from the tenth to the thirteenth centuries at least. The power of the new princes was in part derived from ancient royal rights delegated or usurped, but also from the new realities of vassalage and knights, and their castles riveted their rule upon the land. Of Fulk Nerra, the true founder of the greatness of Anjou, his grandson later recorded that he built thirteen castles which he could list, and others too numerous to name. Such encastellation, which perhaps began at the top of the new society with counts and princes, was not peculiar to the developing county of Anjou but went on similarly and apace in neighbouring principalities, including the Ile de France, the royal domain to which the early Capetian kings were in practice largely confined — and Normandy, rapidly developing from its Viking origins in and after 911 to become the most potent of feudal states.

That castles, held by the duke and his vassals, were well established in Normandy long before 1066 admits of no doubt — any more than does C. H. Haskin's statement that Normandy in 1066 was 'one of the most fully developed feudal societies in Europe'. From the middle of the tenth century we know of the castles of Rouen, Bayeux and Ivry, and in the first half of the eleventh of Tillières, Falaise, Le Homme (L'Isle Marie), Cherbourg, Brix and Le Plessis-Grimoult, Cherrueix, Arques and Caen — to name only some of those to which there is explicit

reference in a paucity of written evidence or certain archaeological proof. Nor is there any doubt that castles were introduced into
England and subsequently Britain, along with feudalism, by the
Normans in and after — and in a few particular cases shortly
before — that memorable date 1066. The only castle sites in
England known to date from the pre-Conquest period are those
associated with the so-called 'Norman favourites' of Edward the
Confessor, and they are the marks of a characteristically Norman
exercise in the aristocratic penetration of their neighbours' lands.
(The Norman Conquest, we may say with Freeman, did not begin
in 1066.) Those castles were Hereford, Richard's Castle, Ewyas
Harold and at least one other unnamed in Herefordshire, where
there was a veritable Norman colony under earl Ralph 'the
Timid', King Edward's nephew; and Clavering in Essex, thought
to have pertained to Robert fitz Wimarc.

   Setting these aside, no one working through the sources of the
period can miss the contrast between the virtual absence of
references to castles in England in the first half of the eleventh
century and the plethora of such references after 1066 as the
Normans raised castles throughout the land in a castle-building
programme the scale of which must be unique (Norman Italy
notwithstanding) in the history of the West. Little or none of this
(for example, three castles in London, two in York) would have
been necessary had castles already been a feature of the Old
English kingdom and its society. As it was, the pattern of the
Norman Conquest, which is the imposition of new lordship, may
be traced by the castles which they planted, from Pevensey to
London via Dover, to Norwich and York, Shrewsbury, Hereford
(already there), Exeter and hundreds more. Two quotations must
suffice from the multitude available. 'There were sixteen houses
where the castle sits', says the Domesday Survey for Gloucester,
'and fourteen have been destroyed in the *burgus* of the city'. The
sagacious Orderic Vitalis, writing of the course of the Norman
Conquest some sixty years afterwards, had this to say: 'For the
fortresses which the Gauls call castles had been very few in the
English provinces, and for this reason the English, although
warlike and courageous, had nevertheless shown themselves too
weak to withstand their enemies.'

Fig. 5. The keep of Langeais Castle, Indre-et-Loire, France.

Fig. 6. The keep of Doué le Fontaine Castle, Maine-et-Loire, France.

Fig. 7. The keep of Tattershall Castle, Lincolnshire.

3
The early castle

The two earliest known castle sites in Europe both have stone
buildings surviving which are residential great towers. From this,
much else follows. It is, first, evidently not true that all early
castles were invariably of earthwork and timber construction
only, nor that thereafter a basic development of castles was thus
always a gradual conversion to stone. Fortification in masonry
was in some cases there from the beginning, and timber
fortification could be undertaken very late, as witness Edward I's
'peel' of Linlithgow in Scotland (1302). It is probably a mistake to
distinguish too sharply, as archaeologists are prone to do,
between castles of earthwork and timber and masonry castles, as
though they were two distinct types. Both modes of construction
might be combined in one building, and indeed were always so if
we count — as we should — the fosses, ditches or moats, wet or
dry, of the fully developed stone castle of the late thirteenth and
fourteenth centuries. In any case the role and function of the
castle did not vary with the materials used in its construction, and
nor, as we shall see, did the basic principles of fortification
employed. Lastly, both Langeais and Doué-la-Fontaine have an
embryonic 'great tower', or, as we would say, 'tower keep', which
also was thus there from the beginning as a type of *donjon*,
which, though especially favoured in the twelfth century, would
survive to the end, as witness Tattershall.

Nevertheless, there is plenty of evidence to suggest that
earthwork-and-timber castles predominated in the beginning,
and certainly in England and Wales in and after 1066. Of these
the best known type is the so-called 'motte-and-bailey' castle,
where to the enclosure, fortified by ditch, bank and palisade, of
the bailey, is added the free-standing strongpoint of the 'motte'
— a mound of earth or rock, artificial or partly so, with its own
ditch about its base and a timber palisade about its summit. The
motte usually stands to one side of the bailey but is much more
rarely found entirely within it as at Bramber and Aldingbourne,
both in West Sussex. Occasionally there are two baileys with the
motte between them, as at Windsor and Arundel or Grimbosc in
Normandy. In any event a timber bridge connected the motte
and/or its summit with the bailey, which contained all those
buildings that were required by a seigneurial household and could
not be confined within the limited space of the motte top.

Fig. 8. The motte at Dinan, from the Bayeux Tapestry.

Fig. 9. The motte at Bayeux, from the Bayeux Tapestry.

The motte bore, seemingly in all or most cases, a timber tower within its palisade. That tower thus became, with the motte, the dominant feature of the castle, the *pièce maîtresse*. It might stand, as it were, upon stilts, to allow the defenders to pass under and through it on the fighting platform of the motte's summit, as appears to be depicted at Dinan (Brittany) on the Bayeux Tapestry and as was revealed by archaeology at Abinger in Surrey. It might also be, and probably most often was, the residence of the castle's lord himself. As such it would be elaborate, even luxurious. The Tapestry shows an elaborate and imposing structure on the motte at Bayeux. Scraps and fragments of a mid twelfth-century *dolce vita* were found in excavating the motte at South Mimms (Hertfordshire). The description by Lambert of Ardres of 'the great and lofty house' built upon the motte at Ardres (Pas-de-Calais) by Arnold, its lord, in about 1117 is worthy of repetition. Three storeys high, it was 'a marvellous example of the carpenter's art . . . piling storeroom upon storeroom, chamber upon chamber, room upon room . . . larders and granaries . . . the chapel in a convenient place overlooking all else from high up on the eastern side . . . On the second floor were the residential apartments and common living quarters . . . and the great chamber of the lord and lady, where they slept . . .' and so on.

On occasion the foundations or lower levels of the tower might be carried down to the natural level beneath and within the motte, as was the case at South Mimms and with the stone tower at Farnham (Surrey), both dating from about 1140. In such cases the tower may be thought of as the primary feature and the motte its strengthening adjunct. In all cases, however, the motte, with its towering superstructures of palisade (necessarily with defended gateway), tower and doubtless subsidiary buildings, was the *donjon* of the motte-and-bailey castle — at once the strongpoint, the inner sanctum and the particular symbol of lordship — and was sometimes specifically so called in contemporary records.

So common were castles of the motte-and-bailey type in the England of the first generation after the Norman Conquest and beyond that there can be no county now without one or (many) more sites whose earthworks survive. Even to name a few of the more impressive examples, like Pleshey or Thetford, Ewyas Harold or Ongar, may seem invidious. In innumerable other cases original and early mottes survive beneath the accumulated stonework of later generations, and thus still dominate their respective castles, as, for example, at Arundel, Tamworth, Launceston, York (Clifford's Tower) or most famously at Windsor. Occasionally a motte might be later added to a castle originally without one, as is known to have happened at Castle Neroche. There are two mottes at Lewes and at Lincoln, though such doubling up is rare (and requires explanation, as do the occasional *donjons jumeaux* on the Continent — for example Niort).

The designer of the Bayeux Tapestry (before 1077?), who often employed a kind of symbolism in his architectural scenes, almost

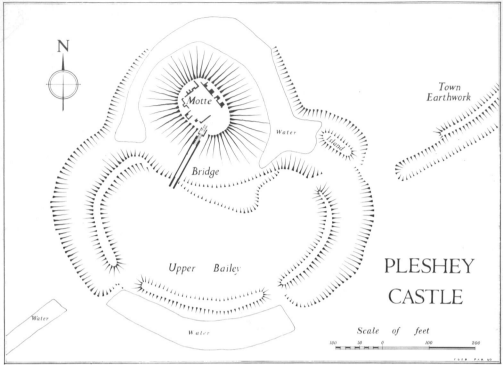

Fig. 10. Ground plan of Pleshey Castle, Essex. (Crown copyright.)

invariably used a motte to represent a castle, apparently irrespective of whether there was one there or not (for example Dinan?). The latest figures from field archaeology, which cannot claim mathematical accuracy, show that of castles raised in England and the Welsh Marches between 1066 and about 1215, 741 had mottes as opposed to 205 without. It is appropriate therefore that on the Tapestry the construction of Hastings, the second castle raised by the Normans after their landing on the Sussex coast in 1066 (the first was at Pevensey), is represented by the raising of the motte. Clearly, the motte-and-bailey castle was or became the preferred type and the near-perfect instrument of conquest and early settlement, comparatively quick and easy to construct, a formidable strongpoint, its motte symbolising lordship. Indeed, the plethora of mottes in Norman England, combined with the embarrassing difficulty of certainly dating any surviving motte in Normandy to the pre-Conquest period by archaeological means, has even led to the suggestion that perhaps the motte-and-bailey type of castle was evolved and invented in the dramatic circumstances of the Norman Conquest of England with its unprecedented castle-building programme. This, howev-

Fig. 11. Aerial view of Pleshey Castle, Essex, photographed from the east. (Crown copyright.)

er, will not do: literary, documentary and types of evidence other than archaeological leave no doubt that the motte and the motte-and bailey castle were established in France and the Rhineland, and in Normandy, before the mid eleventh century.

Nevertheless it is both certain and well known that not all early castles in France, Normandy or England were of the motte-and-bailey type even if constructed exclusively of earthwork and timber. For one thing, some seeming 'mottes' turn out on closer inspection to be inner enclosures, separated from main bailey by their own bank and ditch, their superstructures fallen in and combined with erosion to make them look now like mounds. Of such, Castle Acre may serve as a particularly dramatic example. Secondly, some early castles appear to have had neither motte nor a not dissimilar but less elevated small inner enclosure, but to have consisted simply of a single fortified *enceinte*. The most obvious way to defend anything, whether township or residence, is to put a ring of fortification about it, and Mrs Armitage suggested long ago that this may have been the earliest form of castle. One of the earliest known and visible castle sites in Normandy to be securely dated (before 1047, when it was

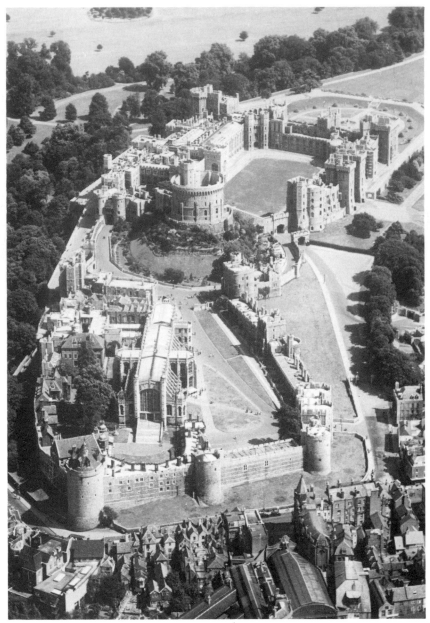

Fig. 12. Aerial view of Windsor Castle, Berkshire.

Fig. 13. Aerial view of Portchester Castle, Hampshire.

abandoned), at Le Plessis-Grimoult, consisted basically of only one fortified enclosure, and so did many of the castles planted by the Normans in England, including the first to be raised in 1066 at Pevensey. There the castle (whose tower keep of curious design was added only in the twelfth century) comprised an enclosure cut out of the larger enclosure of the Old English burgh and former Roman fortress of *Anderida*, and thus half-sheltered by pre-existing walls. That particular pattern was often repeated, as at Portchester (date uncertain) and Exeter, and even at the Tower of London, where it is now known that the Conqueror's castle in its first phase was merely an enclosure of ditch, bank and presumed palisade, in the south-east angle of the Roman and Anglo-Saxon city walls. At Old Sarum, near Salisbury, the first Norman castle was simply an enclosure, like a bull's eye in the centre of the burgh and former iron age fortress.

Other castles of this enclosure type, with no motte and no known inner enclosure, nor yet a great tower of stone, were also constructed outside towns or cities and in the open country, and of this there are excavated examples at Penmaen in West Glamorgan and (more impressive) Barnard Castle, County Durham. In this present study, the modern term 'ringwork' for such fortified enclosures is avoided as ambiguously making no proper distinction between castles and fortified townships, but since these enclosures nowadays receive so much archaeological attention, not least in England and for this early period, it should be emphasised that the enclosure type of castle is a constant in the history of castles, not only in the beginning but from the beginning to the end, and that one could say (though it were better not) that Caernarvon and Conway, for example, in all their perfection, are really very large 'ringworks'. What has worried the present writer is the apparent absence in such castles of any donjon, like the motte with its superstructures or the stone tower keep, to serve as a strongpoint, containing some of the best accommodation, and the particular symbol of lordship. One may guess that there always was such a nucleus, architecturally marked out as the *pièce maîtresse* (and doubtless with shields and banners displayed) as there certainly was at Caernarvon and Conway, where in each case the inner bailey contained the state apartments of the king and queen.

It is already becoming very difficult — and probably artificial — to leave masonry out of this discussion of early castle types. We have seen stonework present at the beginning of the castle's known and visual history at Doué-la-Fontaine and Langeais, and there taking the form of a great tower or tower keep. Setting

Fig. 14. Scolland's Hall, Richmond Castle (North Yorkshire), photographed from the east.

Fig. 15. The gatehouse of Exeter Castle, Devon.

those aside for the moment, we also find that Le Plessis-Grimoult had a stone curtain wall cresting its bank or ramparts before 1047, strengthened by at least one mural tower and an imposing gate tower also of masonry. Soon after 1047, to quote only examples from Normandy, the Conqueror was walling in the great enclosure of his palatial new castle at Caen (to be the centre of ducal lordship in Lower Normandy), supplying it with a stone gate tower and building stone residential apartments within it, while the castle of his unfaithful uncle at Arques may well have been similarly fortified by about the same date.

In Norman England, too, we find castles fortified in stone from the beginning or as soon as it was possible, as, for example, at Richmond (North Yorkshire) and Ludlow. Both of these castles were of the 'simple' enclosure type, with no mottes and their tower keeps added in the twelfth century; but they both had from the beginning mural or flanking towers of stone and stone gatehouses, while Richmond still possesses, in Scolland's Hall, one of the earliest castle halls of masonry, dating from late in the eleventh century. At Exeter the two-storeyed stone gate tower (of the type of Le Plessis-Grimoult) is one of the earliest pieces of castle architecture in England (1068?), nor was it likely that the Conqueror would long leave his castle in London an affair of ditch, bank and palisade. The great White Tower, that is *the* 'Tower of London', was soon inserted, and Rufus built a wall around it in about 1097, presumably soon after his father's palatial structure was completed.

The Conqueror's White Tower brings us to the stone tower keeps, the great towers, the most prestigious buildings, perhaps, of secular lordship, already present at Doué-la-Fontaine and Langeais in the tenth century, increasingly a feature of other castles in France before the mid eleventh century (Montbazon, Nogent-le-Rotrou, Mondoubleau) — and in Normandy at Rouen (by the mid tenth century), Bayeux, Ivry (-la-Bataille) and Brionne. In England the White Tower of London measures 118 by 107 feet (36 by 33 m) and is 90 feet (27 m) high without the turrets. It had originally, above a basement similarly divided, two residential floors each comprising great hall, great chamber and chapel, and each provided with fireplaces and garderobes. The present third floor is a late insertion: the second floor, evidently for the king himself, rose through two levels with a mural gallery and was served by the splendid Chapel of St John. (The first floor was served by that chapel's undercroft.) Externally, the near-unique feature of an apsidal projection at the south-east angle in

Fig. 16. Colchester Castle, Essex.

a basically rectangular tower houses the apse of the chapel. At Colchester the Conqueror's great tower was built on the same plan, including the apsidal projection in the same position, but is even bigger. Both were probably modelled upon the tenth-century great tower of the Norman dukes of Rouen, now vanished. Another stone tower keep of the first generation of the Norman Conquest in England and the marches of Wales stands at Chepstow (later heightened), pertaining to William fitz Osbern, earl of Hereford and the Conqueror's closest friend, and to that we may perhaps add the beginnings of Canterbury and Norwich (both royal).

No one surviving secular monument to the Norman Conquest could be more deliberately impressive than the White Tower of London, and it is also clear that masonry of high quality was present in castles from the beginning in England as in France. Nor could it be otherwise at the hands of the Normans, majestic builders everywhere, who in their duchy in the mid eleventh century were raising the great churches, for example, of Jumièges, Mont-Saint-Michel, and Saint Etienne and La Trinité at Caen, and who, soon after 1066, were to undertake the rebuilding of almost every major church in England on a scale even grander than those in Normandy. The honour of God came first, no doubt, but secular lordship also demanded suitable expression. It may well be that the unique features of the Norman Conquest of England, already stressed, with its urgent need for so many castles so quickly, combined with an unprecedented programme of church building which itself imposed immense demands upon the building industry, enforced a greater than usual reliance upon earthwork and timber fortification in the first generation or so of the conquest, and that this has affected the thinking of English archaeologists and historians ever since.

Be that as it may, an increasing conversion of existing timber defences and buildings to stone was evidently the theme of castle works in England and the marches of Wales in the later eleventh century and throughout the twelfth, and a writ of King John directed in 1204 to the sheriff of Worcester, ordering him to rebuild the castle gateway 'which is now of wood with good and

Fig. 17. Guildford Castle, Surrey. The motte and tower keep.

Fig. 18. Pickering Castle, North Yorkshire. The motte and shell keep.

fine stone', may serve as a text for the process. That process (to be discussed in more detail below) involved the construction of ever more elaborate curtain walls, strengthened by mural towers and gate towers, about the whole perimeter of the castle, the rebuilding in stone of the accommodation within (hall, chambers, chapel, and so on), and the addition very often, especially in the twelfth century, of a great tower. Where such a great tower or tower keep was built in association with a pre-existing motte there might be difficulties: at Norwich the tower could be built upon the gigantic mound, but at Clun and Guildford it had to be cut in to reach the firm foundations of the natural ground. The conversion of an early motte-and-bailey castle to stone more normally involved the construction on or about the motte of a so-called 'shell keep', that is a ring-wall to replace the original palisade, and containing such buildings as the residence of the lord required. Examples are as innumerable as mottes themselves, but the shell keep at Restormel is particularly informative as to the disposition of the surviving residential buildings within it. Other good and straightforward specimens survive at Berkhamsted, Carisbrooke, Arundel and Pickering, though, as we shall see, the shell keep on its motte could become a formidably complex structure, scarcely, if at all, less impressive as a donjon than the great stone tower.

4
The development of the castle

The early castle so far described, whether constructed, over and above its earthworks, of timber or masonry, or both, already displayed all the principles of medieval military architecture (which were largely those of the classical period continued or revived). The enclosure and the tower were present and so were the necessarily strengthened and heavily defended gateway and the techniques of wall walks and flanking fire. What happened next was a development in detail and an increasingly sophisticated application of inherited principles and techniques, rather than any revolutionary change, until an apogee was reached, arguably in the late thirteenth and early fourteenth centuries. So great was the number of castles raised in England and Wales in the first generations of the Norman conquest and settlement ('the first century of English feudalism', let us say), that thereafter new castles on new sites are comparatively rare and the result of particular reasons (Edward I's great castles in north Wales, to forward and hold down the acquisition of new territory, being a classic example). The overall number of castles in the realm decreased rather than increased after, say, the 1150s, and the typical architectural history of the typical English castle is of continuous development on the same early site.

The pattern of development of castle architecture will not fit the mould imposed by that of ecclesiastical architecture. All our terms of reference in medieval architectural history — Romanesque, Gothic, Early English and the rest — are derived exclusively from churches, and cannot, or should not, be applied to castles. It follows also that in castles there is a continuity of development not to be found in churches, where one style gives way to the next, and certainly there is no dramatic transition comparable to that from Romanesque to Gothic. When the Romanesque style of church building reached its apogee at Durham or Lessay at the close of the eleventh century, to be replaced by something different at Saint Denis or Chartres, castles still had two centuries of continuous development before reaching the high point of Caernarvon or Beaumaris, Conway or Harlech.

The tower keep
In tracing this development in its several parts we may begin

Fig. 19. Rochester Castle, Kent.

with the tower keep, though noting first that the word 'keep' is a sixteenth-century coinage, not contemporary, and that for contemporaries this was the 'great tower' or (one form of) 'donjon'. We have met it from the beginning at Doué-la-Fontaine and Langeais, and in Britain at London, Colchester, Chepstow and elsewhere, and already in those prototypes we can distinguish two sorts, the towers proper and those less elevated and thus more oblong, like Langeais and Chepstow, which one may think of perhaps as derived from the first-floor hall. (The Norman historian William of Poitiers referred to the donjon of the castle of Brionne as a stone hall, *aula lapidea.)*

One of the best examples of the developed twelfth-century rectangular tower keeps stands at Rochester and is securely dated to the years following 1127. It was built by Archbishop William de Corbeil with the licence of Henry I, of whom he held the castle. Uncompromisingly a tower, it has three residential floors (rising through four levels) above a basement and measures 70 feet (21.3 m) square with a height of 113 feet (34.4 m) from ground level to parapet, plus a further 12 feet (3.7 m) for the corner turrets. It is of immense but chiefly passive strength, its walls 12 feet (3.7 m) thick at the base narrowing to 10 feet (3.0 m) at the summit. It stands upon a battered plinth or splayed-out base for still greater security, and the great building (like the White Tower and Colchester) is divided by a crosswall or spine-wall from top to bottom to give it greater rigidity. This also facilitates the problem of roofing and automatically provides at each level the division of the internal space into the two basic requirements of seigneurial living, the great hall and the great chamber. Each of the three residential floors has also a small subsidiary chamber in the north-west angle. The second floor provides the grandest residential suite, rising through two levels with a mural gallery around it for extra height and light, and here the crosswall is pierced by an arcade. The third and topmost residential floor evidently had a chapel in at least the eastern half of its main southern division, though this has almost vanished in the rebuilding which followed the siege of 1215, when King John's miners brought down a huge section of the great tower in this south-eastern quarter. Throughout (save in the basement, and there appear to be no garderobes in the top floor) the careful provision of fireplaces and garderobes is a clear indication of residential purpose, and here at Rochester the well shaft is ingeniously brought up, centrally through the crosswall, to serve each floor for greater domestic convenience. Two vices or spiral staircases in two of the corner turrets connect each level from basement to roof, and Rochester also has a forebuilding covering the entrance — with a grand entrance vestibule at first-floor level and a chapel above directly serving the main residential and second floor — a feature which became standard in the major twelfth-century rectangular tower keeps but is generally absent from the earlier examples as at London and Colchester.

The great rectangular keep at Dover, built for Henry II in the 1180s, is even bigger and grander than Rochester and is often represented as the ultimate development of its type. It measures

Fig. 20. The keep of Dover Castle, Kent, with its forebuilding.

Fig. 21. The tower keep at Newcastle upon Tyne, Tyne and Wear.

98 by 96 feet (29.9 by 29.2 m) above the splayed plinth at its base
and excluding the elaborate forebuilding. Its walls are immensely
thick, varying from 21 feet (6.4 m) at the base to 17 feet (5.2 m) at
the top, and it rises to an overall height of 95 feet (29.0 m). Its
internal arrangements are of two residential floors above a
basement for storage, each divided into the two main apartments
by the crosswall, and with subsidiary mural chambers. Of the two
residential floors, the second is much the grander and was clearly
for the king. Again it rises through two levels with a mural
gallery, though greatly mutilated by the brick 'bomb-proof
arches' inserted in the Napoleonic period. There are two chapels,
both in the forebuilding, one at first-floor and the other at
second-floor level, the upper the finer of the two. There is an
ample provision of fireplaces and garderobes, though the former,
like the doorways and window openings, were altered in the later
fifteenth century when the great tower was 'modernised' for
Edward IV. An original feature was a piped water supply served
from a well chamber at the top of the forebuilding.

Rochester has close affinities with Castle Hedingham, built at
about the same time by Aubrey de Vere, presumably to mark his
elevation to the earldom of Oxford in 1141; and Dover has close
affinities with Newcastle upon Tyne, another keep of Henry II,
built a few years earlier by the same master mason, Maurice 'the
Engineer'. Henry II was a great builder of rectangular tower
keeps, his known works including those of Scarborough, Bridg-
north and the Peak (Peveril, Derbyshire) as well as Dover and
Newcastle, while he completed the great towers of Bamburgh,
Bowes and Richmond (North Yorkshire). Comparable baronial
keeps of the mid to late twelfth century include those of Castle
Rising (about 1138), Middleham, Bungay and Norham, the first
two being of the less elevated and more oblong type as found
originally at Chepstow (before its later heightening) and
Langeais.

The rectangular tower keep was thus very much in vogue in the
twelfth century, but nevertheless there was some variation, if not
development, in shape and planning which is especially concentrated towards the close of that century and in the earlier decades
of the thirteenth. This is often represented by historians as
progress and a deliberate change from rectangular to cylindrical
for the elimination of blind angles in defence, with anything in
between — polygonal, quadrilobe, and so on — labelled as
'transitional'. However, it seems to be more a matter of
experiment, preference, fashion, and in some cases even the

Fig. 22. The tower keep of Peveril Castle, Derbyshire.

availability of building materials, since the right angles of rectangular buildings require dressed stone. The known chronology of securely dated tower keeps will not allow a logical progression from rectangular to round via transitional, since the rectangular great tower continued triumphantly to the end of the middle ages (for example Tattershall in England, or Vincennes near Paris) and some of the cylindrical keeps were very early, built long before the full development of their rectangular rivals — for example Fréteval (about 1140?) and Château-sur-Epte (about 1130), both in France, and New Buckenham (about 1146) in England. Some of the so-called transitional towers are comparatively early also. Thus Henry II in England built the polygonal keep at Orford (about 1165-76: compare Chilham and Tickhill, both from the 1170s) before his splendid rectangular great tower at Dover, while the curiously shaped Houdan and

Fig. 23. The oblong tower keep of Castle Rising, Norfolk.

Fig. 24. The polygonal tower keep of Orford Castle, Suffolk.

Etampes in France, the former cylindrical with cylindrical buttresses and the latter quadrilobe, not only pertain to the first half of the twelfth century but also are scarcely 'transitional' from rectangular to round since they are a development from the latter.

Perhaps the most dramatic of the experimentally shaped keeps are the rare specimens *en bec* or beaked, three-quarters cylindrical but with a sharp and solid prow like a ship. Philip II 'Augustus' built the splendid example of La Tour Blanche at Issoudun in about 1202. Richard I's donjon at Château-Gaillard (1196-8) is even more sophisticated with a machicolated war-head (now gone: for machicolation see below and compare Niort, Deux Sêvres) carried on the wedge-shaped corbels which fan out from it; and a more primitive version survives at La Roche Guyon nearby, again by Philip Augustus, about 1190. Philip II's particular preference, however, was evidently for the great cylindrical donjons, which he raised at Dourdan, Châteaudun, Falaise, Verneuil, Lillebonne, Gisors and Rouen, and these, especially when added to castles acquired in Normandy and elsewhere from the Angevins, seem to have been a deliberate symbol of his lordship.

Cylindrical donjons are fewer in Britain and tend to be confined to Wales and the Marches (for example Tretower and Pembroke, both early thirteenth century), though they do occur elsewhere. The early specimen at New Buckenham has already been mentioned, and we may add the great tower on the motte at Launceston (early thirteenth-century). Henry III's Wakefield Tower (about 1230) at the Tower of London is in effect a *donjon cylindrique* in the French fashion and contained the king's privy chamber at first-floor level. Conisbrough has a splendid cylindrical great tower (about 1180), albeit with buttresses. There are no known keeps *en bec* in England or Wales (though the sophisticated shape occurs at Dover in the Norfolk Towers and the Fitzwilliam Gate of the early thirteenth century) and nothing quadrilobe except and until Henry III's Clifford's Tower raised between 1245 and about 1270 on the Conqueror's motte at York (though there was a trefoil keep at Pontefract in the thirteenth century).

Keeps of circular, polygonal or downright peculiar shape do not so obviously lend themselves to the buttresses and forebuildings of rectangular examples, nor to an internal crosswall. Internally there is, in general, less space for ingenious domestic planning beyond one noble room on each residential floor. It may

Fig. 25. The cylindrical, buttressed keep of Conisbrough Castle, South Yorkshire.

be, indeed, that truly palatial keeps of the type of Dover and the Tower of London (*arx palatina* was the phrase used for the latter by William fitz Stephen in the twelfth century), with their self-contained suites of princely accommodation on each residential floor, are less a feature of the later middle ages; but that the tower keep in one form or another survived as a preferred type of donjon, and did not become obsolete from about 1200 as sometimes stated, is sufficiently shown not only by the continued use of those existing but by new ones built, right through to the end of the fifteenth century — as witness those surviving at, for example, Flint, Knaresborough, Nunney, Dunstanburgh, Raglan, Tattershall and Ashby-de-la-Zouch (the last 1474-83). Nor is this surprising. If a fortified residence, a strong house, is required, one method, although less obvious than putting a strong enclosure around the various elements of hall, chamber, chapel and kitchen, is to bring as many as possible of those elements into one defensible unit. The result will be a tower, especially if we add the symbolism of towers and the prestige which high-rise living evidently conferred in the middle ages.

Fig. 26. The cylindrical keep of Pembroke Castle, Dyfed.

Fig. 27. Clifford's Tower, York.

There is no need to distinguish, as has sometimes been done, between the tower keeps of the twelfth century and the so-called 'tower houses' of the later centuries as though both were not in essence the same thing. And to that dominant category of medieval military architecture, though lower down the social scale, the pele towers of northern England, the product of endemic warfare with the Scots from the fourteenth to the sixteenth centuries, obviously belong.

The shell keep

It is probable that the so-called shell keep would repay some of the study more commonly devoted to the great tower. It is usually regarded as particularly a product of the twelfth century and of the conversion of the motte-and-bailey castle to stone, but Edward I seems to have built one on the pre-existing motte at Builth, Totnes is dated to the fourteenth century and the shell keep at Windsor was refurbished with splendid timber-framed apartments (still there) for Edward III. Nor are all so simple — a ring-wall housing buildings built against it — as the type of Trematon or Windsor. Some, like Launceston, Tretower, Farnham and Gisors — and perhaps more than we know — contained a tower keep within them, as we suppose a timber tower commonly rose within the palisade on the motte of old. A similar combination of shell and tower exists, for example, at Castle

Fig. 28. Aerial view of the shell keep and mural tower of Restormel Castle, Cornwall.

Acre, where it is difficult to call the inner enclosure anything but a shell keep though it does not stand upon a motte. Other shell keeps have mural towers set in their circuit, like Lewes or Tamworth or Restormel, and one of these may be an entrance tower or forebuilding as at Arundel, Carisbrooke and Berkhamsted. At this point one may be reminded of the 'seven towers of the Percys' at Alnwick, or of the towering complex that once stood at Sandal, where what seems to have been an elaborate shell keep (or a cylindrical structure open in the centre), with flanking towers, a projecting gatehouse and a great barbican tower thrust out in front of that again, had one of its towers rebuilt in polygonal fashion as late as about 1485. Certainly such a donjon as dominated the castle at Sandal or Alnwick, or at Launceston with its motte, mantlet, 'shell' and tower within, yielded nothing in grandeur, nor residential splendour, to the better known and perhaps more favoured tower keep.

Curtain walls and mural towers

Perhaps no development in medieval military architecture is more obvious and important than the increasingly sophisticated use of projecting mural towers to provide flanking fire (the word

Fig. 29. The complex keep and motte of Launceston Castle, Cornwall. (Crown copyright.)

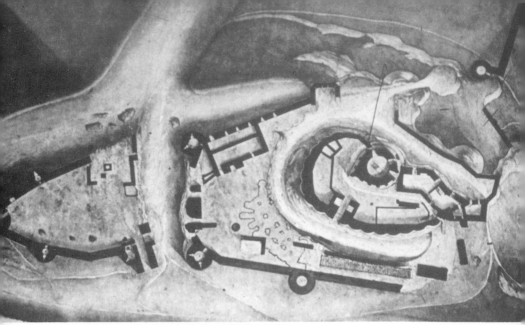

Fig. 30. Ground plan of Château-Gaillard, France.

is inappropriate) upon the exposed outer face of curtain walls. The principle was there from the beginning, as witness archaeological evidence of timber towers at Hen Domen or the early stone towers of the first generation at Richmond and Ludlow, and was in any case derived from Roman practice (as at Portchester). The defence of the whole perimeter of a castle was a fundamental necessity in every case, for no great tower or other keep could be so ingeniously devised as to contain all the requirements of a great seigneurial household, including horses, and thus stand alone. Mural towers not only afforded flanking cover but also rose above the wall head to guard it against assault by escalade, and as a series of strongpoints they divided the curtain, as it were, into sealed sections. The castle being a fortified residence with a near-insatiable need of accommodation, mural towers also provided further residential quarters (no mural tower at the Tower of London is or was without its chambers). As with tower keeps, we see changing fashion in shape, the rectangular towers of the eleventh and twelfth centuries giving way to D-shaped and cylindrical ones in the thirteenth century especially, yet rectangular towers were found again in the latter middle ages (Pickering). Experimental shapes of every kind are also found occasionally, including polygonal (Dover, Avranches Tower; Tower of London, Bell Tower), towers *en bec* (Dover: compare Loches and Gisors), and most notably at Provins (town wall) where it is almost as if a competition were held, each master mason striving to be different. The ultimate exploitation of the principle of flanking fire is to be found about the inner bailey of Richard I's Château-Gaillard (1196-8), where the curtain wall, instead of being set with mural towers, is itself constructed as a series of contiguous semicircular projections.

In terms of surviving military architecture in England, the earliest instance of a complete system of mural towers is Henry II's Dover (1180s), around the inner bailey and that part of the outer curtain which he built (north and east), and the near-

Fig. 31. Ground plan of the keep and inner bailey of Dover Castle, Kent. (Crown copyright.)

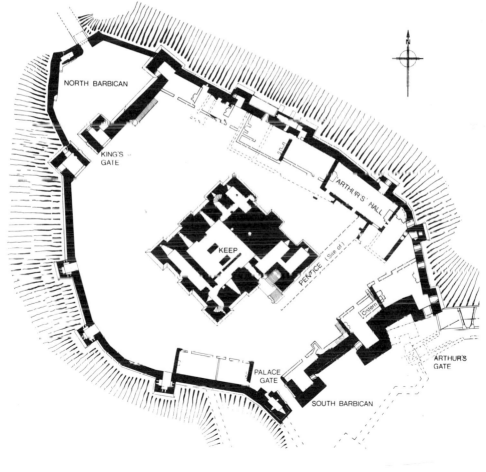

Fig. 32. Dover Castle, Kent. The mural towers of the inner bailey, surrounding the keep.

contemporary castle of Framlingham (the Bigod earl of Norfolk) has a systematic series of very similar rectangular towers, open to the gorge, though both use a polygonal tower at a particularly awkward angle. From then on mural towers are *de rigueur*, binding the whole castle together into one defensible whole, and reach their ultimate in the overwhelming concentration of shooting power at, say, the north end of Dover (early thirteenth century), or the tremendous structure of Marten's Tower at Chepstow (1270-1300), or Caerphilly (late thirteenth century), or the south front of Caernarvon (begun 1283), where there are shooting galleries along the length of the walls as well as in the intermediate stages of the towers.

Concentric defences

The mention of Caerphilly reminds us of the concentric castle and concentric fortification — one line within another, and the former overtopping the latter — generally associated with the period of Edward I, and, for no very good reason, with that king himself, although the *locus classicus* may well be his Beaumaris. It was also by Edward I that the Tower of London was developed into the great concentric castle that it has been ever since, but Caerphilly (the Clare earl of Hertford and Gloucester and lord of Glamorgan) is as good an example as either, and the principle of concentric fortification goes back at least as far as Henry II's

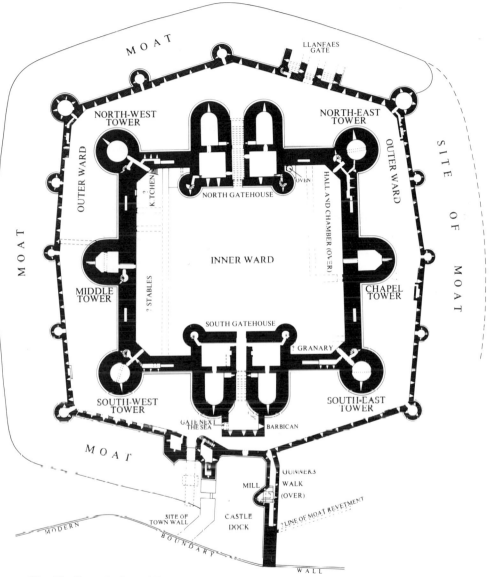

Fig. 33. Ground plan of Beaumaris Castle, Gwynedd. (Crown copyright.)

Dover or Richard I's Château-Gaillard, or further if one includes
eleventh-century Bramber with its motte within its bailey. The
concentric castle is sometimes loosely equated with the 'Edwardian' castle, but the truth is that the technique was used as
necessary, in Edwardian or other times. The chosen sites of
Caerphilly or Beaumaris had no natural advantages, whereas
Conway and Caernarvon were placed on the natural rock with
neither need nor space for concentricity.

Gatehouses
   The entrance to the castle being a potential weak point, its
fortification received much attention during the middle ages and
the development of the gatehouse is a major theme in the study of
castles. Setting aside those entrances which are simply a gateway
through the curtain wall, albeit usually defended by an adjacent
tower (Richmond may have been an early example and Conway
is a late one), the earliest form of gatehouse proper is evidently a
single tower of at least two storeys, pierced by the entrance
passage, of the type of Le Plessis-Grimoult (before 1047), Exeter
(about 1068) or Castle Rising (about 1138). While the single-
tower gatehouse may continue late, as witness Leeds, Kent
(remodelled by Edward I), in England what are prototypes of
something more impressive and more characteristic of the later
middle ages survive at Dover in the two gateways of Henry II's
inner bailey, the King's Gate and the Palace Gate, where in each
case two of the rectangular mural towers of the curtain are
brought in close on either side of the entrance passage. From here
the way seems straight, via for example Beeston (1220s) or
Edward I's Middle and Byward gates at the Tower of London, to
the great twin-towered gatehouses of the 'Edwardian' and later
periods, as at Caerphilly, Tonbridge, Harlech, Beaumaris and
elsewhere. Paradoxically, these have become so strong that the
term 'keep-gatehouse' has been coined for them, and they
contain in their upper levels some of the best residential
accommodation, not least at Harlech and in the two gatehouses at
Beaumaris. In the majestic King's Gate at Caernarvon (about
1300), which is the main and state entrance to the castle from the
town, almost all the defensive devices and techniques known to
the period were used in multiplicity. There was first an outer
drawbridge across the northern moat and then no less than five
great doors and six portcullises before an inner drawbridge (never
completed). The passageway itself was intended to have a
right-angled turn and was covered throughout by lateral arrow

Fig. 34. The twin-towered gatehouse of Caerphilly Castle, Mid Glamorgan.

slits and spyholes at various levels and no less than nine (perhaps more) *meurtrières* or murder-holes above.

Portcullis, drawbridge, barbican, machicolation and other details

The portcullis or heavy iron grill to be raised and lowered in front of gates is a well known castle feature, and arrow slits and *meurtrières* are self-explanatory. The drawbridge, technically a turning bridge or *pont levis*, usually working by counterweights, though an ancient device, is scarcely ever found incorporated in the structure of stone gatehouses before the late thirteenth century. Almost the only defensive techniques not to be employed at Caernarvon (which may be thought not to need any more) are the barbican or outwork in front of the gate (compare Edward I's so-called Lion's Tower at the Tower of London and the similar and contemporary half-moon barbican at Goodrich) and machicolation. Machicolation, a corbelled-out projecting gallery about the head of towers, gate towers especially, and less often walls, to facilitate the defence of the outer face and foot, seems perhaps to have been more popular in France than the English kingdom, though fine examples can be found at Nunney (fourteenth-century and very 'French'), Raglan (fifteenth cen-

Fig. 35. Exterior and sectional views of a drawbridge. (From Viollet-le-Duc, *Dictionnaire Raisonné de l'Architecture.*)

tury) and elsewhere. It is, however, only a version in masonry of the far older timber hoarding which could once have been found crowning many an English and Anglo-Norman tower (for example, the joist holes still about the keep at Rochester) and evidently still survives at Stokesay.

Residential buildings

The castle being always a lordly fortified residence, there was no less concentration, as the centuries proceeded, upon its more outright residential buildings (as opposed to the accommodation afforded by keeps and towers) than upon any other part. Indeed, nothing can more strongly emphasise the castle's true social function than that most of Edward III's prodigious expenditure upon Windsor between 1350 and 1377 (£51,000 and the highest recorded for any single building operation in the whole history of English medieval royal works) was spent upon the provision of splendid state apartments for the king and queen in the upper bailey and the establishment of the Order of the Garter and the first St George's Chapel in the lower. Windsor, his birthplace (he was Edward 'of Windsor'), was to be the particular centre of and setting for the king's court and chivalry, the Versailles of the age. Among non-royal castles, the virtual rebuilding of Kenilworth

Fig. 36. Exterior and sectional views of hoarding. (From Viollet-le-Duc, *Dictionnaire Raisonné de l'Architecture.*)

Fig. 37. Exterior and sectional views of machicolation. (From Viollet-le-Duc, *Dictionnaire Raisonné de l'Architecture.*)

(except the keep) by John of Gaunt in much the same period was largely devoted to the construction of magnificent ranges of domestic apartments to west and south, including the present ruined hall. The supreme surviving castle chapel in England must be the present fifteenth-century St George's Chapel, again at Windsor.

The quadrangular castle

Of the development of the residential buildings within the castle only a few particularly impressive examples have been given, but in it all can be seen little more than changing architectural style and fashion. It would be reckless to assume that at this level of society the style of living became grander in the later middle ages, for it was grand before. We do see something new, however, in the total architectural integration of

Fig. 38. The remains of supports for machicolation at Nunney Castle, Somerset.

the residential and military roles of the castle into one planned and unified structure in the quadrangular castles of the fourteenth and fifteenth centuries. The arrangement of residential buildings about a quadrangle had for many centuries been the norm in monasteries, and there were residences arranged on the quadrangular plan even within castles in certain cases from the twelfth century onwards (Sherborne, Old Sarum, Henry II's Windsor and John's 'Gloriette' at Corfe), but the quadrangular castle with all its lavish accommodation as part of one articulated whole was something different and finds its finest exposition at Bolton-in-Wensleydale and Bodiam, both of the later fourteenth century. Bodiam exploited the technique of broad water defences (compare Leeds in Kent, Kenilworth, and Caerphilly above all), which, second only to building on natural rock, was the best safeguard against undermining. Nevertheless, neither Bodiam nor Bolton was amongst the strongest castles in the land. Bolton especially suggests the fortified manor house rather than the castle proper ready to resist the full force of war, and this was certainly the case with some of the later examples of the quadrangular type, like Baconsthorpe (mid fifteenth-century), Herstmonceux (about 1440), Hever (about 1482) and Oxburgh Hall (about 1480 and never called a castle).

Fig. 39. Bodiam Castle, East Sussex. Built in quadrangular form and using water defences.

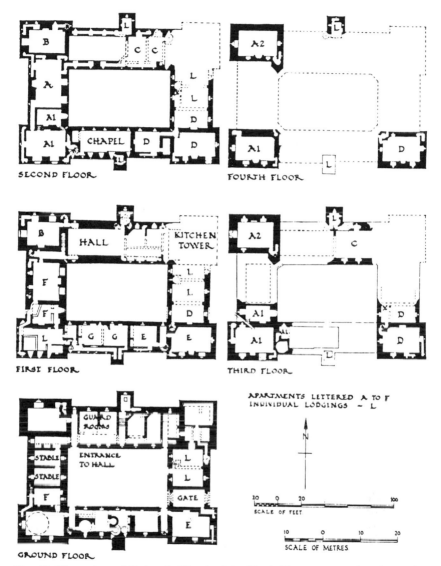

Fig. 40. Floor plans of Bolton-in-Wensleydale, North Yorkshire, showing the castle's accommodation.

5
The decline of the castle

What happened to the castle in the end was precisely this lowering of the guard, the falling away of its military importance, to leave the unfortified great house and stately residence. At approximately the same time the appearance of the exclusively military coastal forts of the Tudors advertised, as it were from the other side, the breaking of that unique combination of lordly residence and fortress which made the castle and made it peculiarly feudal. To discuss the decline of the castle is to discuss change in the whole nature of society, the slow evolution of the modern territorial nation state. As much work still needs to be devoted to later castles as has been given to early castles and their origins. Meanwhile we can at least be cautious and careful not to over-simplify. The secular princes and aristocracy of the feudal period did not live exclusively in castles. There were always some unfortified palaces like royal Westminster and Clarendon, or hunting lodges like Brill and Woodstock. There were always also those half-way houses, lightly fortified, between the castle and the civil residence, of the sort if not the appearance of those fortified manors which we too easily associate with the fifteenth century. Domesday Book (1086) refers to *domus defensabiles*, and Stokesay, Acton Burnell and Little Wenham are surviving examples from the thirteenth century and the apogee of castle building. There are also a great many moated sites in Yorkshire and East Anglia which, like many 'pele towers' of the north, were never intended to be castles. At this level considerations of domestic security rather than aristocratic pretensions and the panoply of war are motivations, and one may be reminded of Patrick Forbes building Corse Castle in Aberdeenshire in about 1500 — 'Please God, I will build me such a house as thieves will knock at ere they enter.' We must remember, before hastening to write off castles along with feudalism, that many still had a gallant role to play in the seventeenth-century Civil War (the 'Great Rebellion'), and also that aristocratic military tradition lingered on, to find architectural expression in a splendid new castle at Peckforton as late as the mid nineteenth century. The decline of the castle did not follow at once upon the introduction of gunpowder into warfare in about 1300. For some two hundred years its only noticeable effect was the provision of gunports in addition to arrow slits for the castle's own defence.

Fig. 41. Stokesay Castle, Shropshire. A fortified residence of the thirteenth century.

Further reading

Armitage, E. S. *Early Norman Castles of the British Isles*. John Murray, 1912 (and reprints).

Brown, R. Allen. *The Architecture of Castles : a visual guide*. Batsford, 1984.

Brown, R. Allen. *English Castles*. Batsford third edition, 1976.

Renn, D. F. *Norman Castles in Britain*. John Baker, 1968.

Acknowledgements

The publishers acknowledge the assistance of Mr William L. Gates in the selection of illustrations for this book. Illustrations are reproduced with the kind permission of: Aerofilms Ltd, fig. 12; Her Majesty's Stationery Office, figs. 11, 29, 31, 33; Cadbury Lamb, figs. 1, 16, 17, 18, 19, 20, 21, 22, 24, 26, 27, 32, 38 and front cover; Ministry of Defence, fig. 10; the Royal Archaeological Institute, fig. 40; Geoffrey N. Wright, fig. 14. Figs. 3, 4, 5, 6, 7, 13, 15, 23, 25, 28, 30 and 34 are from the author's collection.

56

Index

Page numbers in italic refer to illustrations